Job Search in the 21st Century

by Bill Meyer

ISBN: 1500999334
ISBN 13: 9781500999339
Library of Congress Control Number: 2014918105
CreateSpace Independent Publishing Platform
North Charleston, South Carolina

Table of Contents

1. Introduction:

This Book Is Unique

I wrote this book because of the colossal changes that have occurred in the world between the middle of the twentieth century and the beginning of the twenty-first century. They have occurred in countries, economies, companies, and people. However, little change has occurred in the way people find jobs in the twenty-first century. The result has been frustration, unemployment, and jobs that do not match people's skills. This book attempts to provide people new job-search skills that will help them find work that matches their objectives in the twenty-first century.

I have experience that includes:
- spending more than forty-five years in business and education as a part of the job-search process;
- publishing articles in the *National Business Employment Weekly*, previously related to the *Wall Street Journal* (articles included "Networking Is Like Growing a Flower Garden," "Cover Letters That Don't Go Clunk," and "Fired at 50: One Executive's Story");
- completing a one-week course in recruiting at McGill University and later teaching the same course at Georgetown University;
- establishing AT&T's Western Region College Recruiting Program;

- cofounding and conducting, with a Silicon Valley executive search consultant, career planning workshops at the Menlo Park Presbyterian Church; and
- providing guidance to students preparing to attend college, students graduating from college, and workers in midcareer.

The book is short. It does not overwhelm the reader with repetitive, unnecessary information. It recommends a new, twenty-first-century approach to a job search. Those recommendations apply to high school and college seniors as well as people in midcareer. The objective of the book is to provide practical information and facts on what works and what does not work. Facts about the current economic environment, which are blended into integrated topics, are sourced from the *New York Times*, the *Wall Street Journal*, *Bloomberg Businessweek*, and other business publications; quality Internet resources; my prior writings; university lesson plans; and experiences and observations.

There is no silver bullet. Finding a good job requires patience, focus, hard work, overcoming rejection, and the courage to do things that may not be comfortable. However, if the reader applies these recommended job-search strategies, I believe he or she will have an advantage in finding a good job in the highly competitive twenty-first century.

I must acknowledge Ms. Leslie Anne Geyer of Carmel, California. Leslie lit the hidden fire that stimulated me to write this book. She has dedicated her life to helping others, both in the United States and overseas, and has a long list of recognitions that attest to her accomplishments.

2.

Jobs Were Plentiful in the Second Half of the Twentieth Century, but Companies and Jobs Were in Transition

When I graduated from college, I had job offers from IBM, Procter & Gamble, AT&T, General Electric, and others. I had my pick; opportunities were great. Things are very different now. There are many reasons for the changes in the twentieth century. They include the following:

The Demise of the US Steel Industry

Because the steel industries in Europe, Russia, and Asia were destroyed during World War II, the world bought steel from US Steel, Bethlehem Steel, National Steel, and so forth. There were no other options. However, over time, foreign steel companies were rebuilt with the newest steelmaking equipment and processes. Unfortunately, the US steel companies did not keep pace and for too long stayed with the steelmaking equipment and processes of the past. Most US steel companies were downsized or went out of business during the twentieth century.

In the twenty-first century, the major foreign steel companies, based on output, include Arcelor Mittal (headquartered in Luxembourg), Nippon Steel (Japan), POSCO Steel (South Korea), Tata Steel (India), and seven large steel companies in China.

Today, US Steel ranks thirteenth, and Nucor (a US specialty steel company) ranks fourteenth.

My experience: I worked as a laborer at Laclede Steel in Alton, Illinois, for four summers in the late 1950s. I was also a member of the United Steelworkers of America. Jobs in the steel industry were plentiful, but it was tough, dangerous work.

The Information Technology Industry
IBM
From the late 1950s until the late 1980s, IBM ruled the information technology roost. Almost all companies used IBM mainframe computers. Information systems vice presidents would often say, "You will never get fired by buying from IBM." Many of the best and brightest students, therefore, flocked to work for IBM.

The chairman and chief executive officer (CEO) of IBM was smart, ethical, and handsome. However, he was imbued with IBM traditions including "employment for life," and so forth. Then things changed. Bill Gates established Microsoft. It provided software for personal computers (PCs). Dell, Hewlett-Packard, and others provided the hardware that ran on Microsoft's Windows operating system. Suddenly, IBM's mainframe approach to computing became less desirable, and IBM started a dive toward insolvency.

Some thought the chairman and CEO of IBM could not find it in his DNA to make the employee reductions and other changes required to keep IBM afloat. Then the unthinkable happened: an IBM outsider was hired as the CEO in 1993 and served until 2002. He took the necessary steps to keep the company going, including reducing the number of employees, and was largely credited with turning IBM's fortunes around. In the process, IBM became a much smaller company.

Hewlett-Packard (HP)

HP was recognized during the twentieth century for its research and product development. Research at HP Labs led to innovative new products—as research at Apple does today. HP's products were often the first of their kind. As an example, in 1972 HP developed the world's first handheld scientific calculator, the HP-35. It sold for $400. (Today one can buy a scientific calculator for $10 to $20.) HP sold 100,000 35s in 1972 and 300,000 before it was discontinued in 1975, as many competitors entered the market.

Then things suddenly changed because of issues with HP's board of directors. A series of CEOs were quickly hired and fired, and questionable acquisitions were made. Today, one of HP's main products is commodity-priced PCs, primarily through the purchase of Compaq Computer. HP is no longer the premier job-growth company it once was. On October 6, 2014, HP announced it would split into two companies and reduce the number of employees.

The Telecommunications Industry

Until 1984, AT&T (or the Bell System) was the telecommunications industry. It was a giant. It consisted of AT&T Corporation, AT&T Long Lines Department, Bell Telephone Laboratories, Western Electric, Sandia Corporation, and twenty-three local Regional Bell Operating Companies (RBOCs). It was the largest nongovernmental employer in the United States.

However, in 1984, everything changed. AT&T signed a consent decree with the US Department of Justice. It was based on an antitrust lawsuit alleging that the Bell System companies were using illegal practices to stifle competition in the telecommunications industry. The results of the consent decree were as follows:

- AT&T Corporation and its Long Lines Department were allowed to continue as one unit.
- Bell Laboratories and Western Electric morphed into or merged with other companies.
- Southwestern Bell Telephone Company, one of the largest RBOCs, gradually absorbed many of the other RBOCs. It eventually bought what was left of the existing AT&T and renamed itself AT&T.
- Competition between the new AT&T and many newly formed competitors required a reduction in the number of the remaining AT&T employees.

My experience:
- In the late 1950s and early 1960s, AT&T and its twenty-three local telephone companies employed over 120,000 telephone operators. However, by the mid-1980s, AT&T had almost no telephone operators. When a customer made a call, he or she connected directly to digital switching systems; operators were no longer required.
- During the mid-1980s, AT&T implemented remote, centralized testing systems. These systems significantly improved customer service. However, they also reduced the number of employees required to perform local testing functions.
- Until the mid-1960s, all equipment in cable and microwave systems used vacuum tubes. The company converted to solid-state equipment, which was more reliable, lasted longer, and was less expensive. However, this also reduced the number of employees.
- Between the 1920s and today, AT&T converted from copper-wire systems to light-wave systems. That conversion dramatically reduced the cost per circuit mile but also reduced the number of people required to maintain those systems.

In summary, new technology permitted AT&T to provide better service at less expense, but with fewer employees as well.

The Automobile Industry

In the twentieth century, there were many automobile companies in the United States. They included General Motors (GM), Ford, and Chrysler. They also included many others, such as Packard, LaSalle, Studebaker, Nash, Pierce Arrow, Hudson, and Kaiser. These others stopped making automobiles because of bankruptcy or mergers.

By the middle of the twentieth century, only two US car companies remained: GM and Ford. Chrysler was purchased by Fiat (although Chrysler cars are still being manufactured in the United States), partly because of competition from Toyota, Honda, Mercedes Benz, BMW, Hyundai, and others.

GM almost went bankrupt in 2007–2008, and the US government provided $50 billion to keep the company afloat. GM eliminated many brands, including Pontiac, Oldsmobile, and SAAB, and closed many manufacturing plants and dealerships. In 1979, the number of GM employees peaked at 853,000 worldwide. In 2008, GM employees worldwide numbered about 266,000.

The Changing Face of the Workforce

The Increase in Women in the Job Market

Forty-five to fifty years ago, most job opportunities for women were as teachers, nurses, and clerks. Most women stayed at home. Today, women are presidents of many US companies, including GM, Hewlett-Packard, and IBM. In addition, many women have become highly educated professionals such as doctors, lawyers, and accountants.

My experience: When I attended Purdue in the late 1950s, about 5 percent of the students were women, and most received degrees in home economics, nursing, or teaching. Today, about 50 percent of women attending Purdue receive degrees in engineering or related technical fields and are highly recruited by many companies.

The Increase in Outsourcing
Many companies have decided that to remain in business, they must outsource their work to other countries with lower costs. Jobs in the United States disappeared and were replaced by jobs in Mexico, China, India, and other nations.

My experience: I worked for SanDisk Corporation as a consultant for two years. During that time, SanDisk outsourced all manufacturing work in the United States to countries in Asia.

The Increase in Foreign Students
There are 40 percent more international college students in the United States today than there were a decade ago. Chinese enrollment increased 21 percent between 2012 and 2013. In 2014, 819,644 international students attended US colleges and universities, including 236,000 from China, 97,000 from India, and 71,000 from South Korea.

The Stagnant US Economy: Fewer Jobs for Graduates
The growth in the US economy has been weak since the deep recession that started in 2007. Increases in the annual gross national product have been below the growth rates before 2007 and may remain so for a long time. The result is that the growth in available jobs is below that experienced before 2007 and may remain historically low for some period.

A 2012 article in *The Atlantic* magazine concluded that 53 percent of college graduates were jobless or underemployed. Other studies, prepared by Drexel University and the Economic Policy Institute and other organizations, reached similar conclusions. In addition, a recent poll by After College, an online entry job site, indicated that 83 percent of college seniors graduated without a job in the spring of 2014.

Some conclude that many educational institutions do not survey their graduated students to determine whether they are employed and, if they are, whether the job they accepted required a college degree. As an example, a 4,000-student survey made in early 2014 by Millennial Branding, a consulting firm, found that 61 percent of the students said that career service organizations were "rarely" or "never" effective in helping them land a job. Therefore, some are now advocating that universities and colleges be required to provide comprehensive job-search skills training for all their students.

However, there are exceptions. Connecticut College, a liberal arts school, offered financial incentives to students who participate in its career-training program, and many students did so. The result is that 96 percent of all Connecticut College alumni report that they either had a job upon graduation or went on to graduate school.

In addition, the Paul Merage MBA Program at University of California, Irvine, surveys their graduating students. In 2013, 88 percent of the full-time graduating class accepted full-time job offers no later than three months after graduation.

My experience: I was an adjunct professor in the School of Business at California State University–Monterey Bay for five years.

I observed many recent graduates who were unemployed or underemployed in jobs that did not require a college degree. Several recent graduates were working as waiters or hostesses at restaurants. One graduate was flipping hamburgers at a local coffee house restaurant. Another was observed sweeping the sidewalk at a curio shop. These situations are not peculiar to Monterey County, California; they exist in almost all parts of the country.

In Summary
Compared to the twentieth century, getting a good job in the twenty-first century's tough job market requires hard work, focus, patience, persistence, and the acquisition of new job-search skills.

3.

Jobs Are Recovering in the Twenty-First Century, but the Rule Book for Jobs and Job-Search Skills Is Changing

Work and job opportunities and company cultures are being transformed in the twenty-first century. The job environment and working conditions will be much different than in the twentieth century. The following describes twenty-first-century trends:

21st century

- Top-down management is out; collaborative and teamwork management is in.
- Large, slow-moving bureaucracies are out; quickly moving organizations are in.
- Work in the office is decreasing; working from home is increasing.
- Hierarchy is out; flat organizations are in.
- Traditional kinds of work are out; new kinds of work are in.
- Forty-hour-per-week jobs are out; contract work, part-time work, and remote-access work are in.
- Compensation and promotions based on seniority and politics are out; compensation and promotions based on measured results is in.
- Traditional and rigid work hours are out; flexible and longer work hours are in.
- Plush offices and long lunches are out; jeans and lunches in the cubicle are in.

- Liberal arts education (with a few exceptions) is out; skill-based education is in.
- Big staffs are out; productive, skill-based jobs are in.
- Employment for life is out; employment with several companies in different jobs is in.
- A college degree in the twenty-first century is like a high school degree in the twentieth century; therefore, continuing and higher education will be required to keep pace.

Most studies indicate the major job growth opportunities in the twenty-first century will be in health care, energy, and information technology.

Health Care
The United States will be meeting the expanding health-care needs of an increasing number of patients—and creating new jobs.
- Despite the controversy, the Affordable Health Care Act will provide health-care coverage to many who previously did not have it.
- The United States is aging, and the number of Americans requiring health care is increasing. In 2009, 12.9 percent of the US population was sixty-five years or older. That percentage is expected to grow to 19 percent by 2030.
- Medical processes and techniques are rapidly improving. They include minimally invasive microsurgery, robotic and remote surgery, and significant improvements in medical equipment.

This situation will result in an increase in the number of jobs for doctors, nurses, physician assistants, hospital administrators, and other health-care providers. In addition, the medical-device industry will expand, which includes the design, manufacturing, and marketing and sales of medical devices. The pharmaceutical industry will also grow, which includes the research and manufacture of drugs and an increase in jobs for pharmacists and related jobs.

Energy

The United States will be meeting the increasing energy needs of the world, which, in turn, will increase the number of new jobs in the United States.

- The October 8, 2014, issue of the *New York Times* had an eight-page special section called "Energy—Reversing the Flow of Oil." The section explained how the United States will transform itself from an energy-importing to an energy-exporting nation. The article made two key points:
  o In 2014, the United States started to export petroleum for the first time in the last forty years. Those exports will increase dramatically in the future.
  o In the next three to five years, the United States will be exporting liquefied natural gas to the world.
- The world is moving toward electric cars. Tesla, the electric car manufacturer, plans to increase the battery capacity of its cars, stepping up its manufacturing, and expanding into new markets, including China. Other companies are also producing both fully electric and partially electric or hybrid cars that increase miles per gallon and reduce air pollution.
- In 2008, according to the Surface Transportation Board, 9,500 railcars were used to move crude oil across the United States. In 2013, 415,000 railcars moved crude oil across the United States. This indicates that the crude oil export business is rapidly growing.
- Some predict the United States will become the world's top energy provider in the next five to ten years, possibly exceeding Russia and Saudi Arabia.

This situation will result in an increase in the number of jobs in petroleum engineering, civil engineering, railroad equipment manufacturing, battery research and design, geology, drilling technology and equipment, and related fields.

Information Technology

Information technology (IT) companies will grow in the United States, which will improve business efficiency and the lives of people and create new jobs. IT is increasing for the following reasons:

- The world is becoming interconnected through the Internet and the use of many new IT applications. As an example, the application Uber permits a customer to hire a taxi, a private car, or ride-share services using a mobile phone.
- Social media services and networks are rapidly growing.
- There is rapid growth in creative IT applications. They include work done by Google, Apple, and many other design and support companies located around Silicon Valley and other high-tech centers in the United States.

The results will include an increase in the number of jobs in information systems research, engineering, programming, product design, and IT marketing and sales.

IT jobs in the twenty-first century will be available to those who acquire or upgrade their skills to "mind work" instead of manual labor. Making that transformation will be a challenge to many and a requirement for all.

Contract and Part-Time Work Will Grow in the Twenty-First Century

Job seekers should consider contract work. Examples of contract work include developing a computer program, managing a project, or applying skills to meet the short-term objectives of a business. Part-time work can be considered a subset of contract work, except that no contract is required and the job may involve less than forty hours a week.

Reasons for the increase in contract work include the following:
- Prior to the economic downturn, some companies would maintain a workforce that could meet the peak-and-valley demands of a company. In today's highly competitive global economy, many companies can no longer do so; they meet peak demand with contract employees.
- A report by a highly respected consulting firm concluded that 58 percent of the companies surveyed stated they would increase their use of contract workers.
- One of the largest employment firms in the country concluded that 50 percent of new jobs that emerge after the recession would be contract jobs.
- An employment agency study concluded that 43 percent of its billable hours in 2013 were for contract work.
- Another employment agency study of employers concluded that 42 percent intend to hire contract employees as part of their staffing strategy in 2014.

Why Some Find Contract Work Desirable
- The job seeker can find work quickly; job placement is fast.
- Work schedules are flexible.
- Contract work provides access to jobs and companies that might not be posted in a local newspaper.
- It may lead to permanent, full-time employment.
- It provides income while the job seeker looks for a permanent job.
- The pay may exceed the hourly rate for similar work done by a regular employee.

Why Some Find Contract Work Undesirable
- The work does not provide the benefits of a permanent employee, such as health insurance and paid vacations.
- Contract work is for a limited period.

4.

Would You Set Sail before You
Knew Where You Wanted to Go?

If you want to sail to another place, first identify where you want to go and how to get there. Otherwise, you may find yourself where you do not want to be. This self-discovery should be the *first part* of the job-search process.

I have worked with students and others in business and as an adjunct professor at both San Francisco State University (business ethics) and California State University–Monterey Bay (business communications). I would often ask these questions: "What kind of work do you want to do? What kind of a degree do you want to acquire?" The answer was often, "I don't know." I often responded by saying, "Most people don't have a clue until they are in their late twenties or early thirties. You have time to determine that."

Sadly, too many people never figure it out or figure it out too late. They get trapped in a job that makes an eight-hour day feel like a sixteen-hour day. In addition, a mortgage and a family make it tough to risk trying something new, so they just survive—miserably.

There is no magic wand that can positively help you identify your work DNA. Career counselors in colleges and universities and in private practice can sometimes help. There are also tests one can take and books one can read. The classic book is *What Color Is Your Parachute?* It was first published in 1970 and is now in its fortieth edition. It's worth the read.

However, there is another way. Ask yourself, "What do I do well and what do I enjoy doing?" As an example, I enjoy playing baseball, but I can't do it well enough to make a job out of it. You may say, "I like books and to classify and store them, but librarians don't make any money." Nevertheless, if you are at the top of your game as a librarian, you may be surprised. The president of the New York City Public Library makes about $800,000 a year.

Then there are those who say, "I want to be a lawyer or real estate agent because they make a lot of money." Don't be misled. There are many lawyers that don't make a lot of money, and only a small percentage of real estate agents actually do. A Gallup survey of 450,000 Americans in 2008–2009 revealed that people found "day-to-day contentment" as their income rose, but beyond $75,000 ($84,000 in 2014), that contentment plateaued. If you make a modest income but you enjoy what you are doing, making a lot of money may not be that important.

Don't get trapped in the notion that you must have a white-collar job because of the alleged prestige. Some people start as plumbers, establish a plumbing business, and then franchise or expand their business. Some of the yachts sitting at the end of long piers in front of mansions in Miami belong to people who started as plumbers.

Knowing When a Job Matches Your DNA
A relative acquired a summer internship and, based on that experience, decided he wanted to work for that company after

graduation. He did not interview with other companies before graduation. Unfortunately, upon graduation, the company did not offer him a job.

He eventually did find a job in his chosen industry. However, after four years, he decided it was not for him and determined he wanted to acquire an MBA in marketing. He got an MBA from a California university and landed a marketing job after graduation. But most marketing work, he discovered, involved doing marketing studies, and he found it boring and unsatisfying: he was, he said, "working with his head down in a cubicle."

Upon reflection, he decided he wanted a job with customer contact where, as he put it, "if I make a sale, I get a piece of the action." He found a job with a software company where he performed direct-contact sales. He gets to work early, stays late, is positively recognized by management, and loves every minute. He has found work that he loves and does well. Within four months, he led the company in his unit for all customer contact sales

What can be learned from his experience?
- If you are about to graduate from college, sign up for interviews with many companies in many fields. In the process, you will hone your interviewing skills, and you may find a job opportunity in a field you had never considered.
- Your first job decision is often wrong. If that happens, leave— but not before you find another job.
- Learn from previous jobs as it may help you identify what matches your DNA; however, do not become an unfocused "job hopper."
- When you find the job that best fits your DNA, you *will* know it. You will want to go to work early and stay late.

Consider Enlisting

However, suppose that, despite your best thinking, you simply don't know what degree you want before enrolling in college. Perhaps you try college for a year or two and then drop out. *Do not* drift aimlessly into repairing tires or flipping burgers. If you do, you may become acclimated to your situation; do not let that happen.

Instead, consider enlisting in the armed forces. The military has some of the finest training schools in the country; however, you must commit to an enlistment contract to attend them. It does *not* mean that you will become engaged in combat—unless you choose to do so, and if you do, consider the army and marines. The Coast Guard attracts those who want a noncombat adventure and want to help people. Both the navy and air force are noted for training people in skills that can apply to the job market after they leave the service. *However, do not* enlist after only one or two visits to a recruiting office or let an armed forces recruiter rush you into enlisting; spend time thinking about it and research the opportunity thoroughly before you do so.

After you complete your commitment, you may have a skill that can be easily transferred to a good job in the civilian sector. You will also be more mature and will have developed leadership skills and self-discipline, and you will be much better prepared to return to college.

My experience: The armed services can positively change your life. It did mine. The navy sent me to college for five years. In return, I spent three years as a navy officer on an aircraft carrier and qualified for officer of the deck for carrier task force operations. Before I accepted a Regular Naval Reserve Officers Training Corps Scholarship, my vision of the world had been limited to Missouri and Illinois. After my three navy midshipman cruises and three-year navy commitment, my vision expanded to include most of Western Europe and Asia. I was transformed into a different person.

5.

Why New Job-Search Skills Are Required in the Twenty-First Century

T he job-search skills that were successful in the twentieth century will not be successful in the twenty-first century. There are many reasons why.

Companies were growing in the second half of the twentieth century. Competition for jobs was not significant. Several companies dominated their markets. Job seekers did not need to contact company recruiters; recruiters came to them. Many job seekers received multiple offers. Jobs were easy to find. It was the "best of times."

However, in the latter half of the twentieth century—and to date in the twenty-first century—all that has changed. Competition for jobs is now very high. Many of the jobs in the twentieth century are gone—never to return. Many students are graduating with degrees that are not required in the twenty-first century.

The result is that companies and their human resource departments are swamped with job inquiries. Some companies do nothing more than process résumés through a scanner that identifies key words. It is the "worst of times."

New job-search skills can help job applicants in the twenty-first century:

- Identify job opportunities by canvassing local business newspapers for articles about "people on the move." Those articles often identify a problem a new manager may have. Write directly to him or her. Tell the manager how you can help solve his or her problem. *Companies want problem solvers.*
- Contact a hiring manager in a company, based on extensive research. It's not done by sending out hundreds of e-mails with one stroke of the Send key or by sending introductory letters and résumés to personnel or human resources.
- Focus your résumé on a brief, concise job objective and solid accomplishments.
- Network, network, and network.
- Prepare, prepare, and prepare for all interviews.

And finally, you must be prepared to put forth much more time and effort in the twenty-first century than in the twentieth century. There is no substitute for hard work—make your job search a campaign.

6. Recruiters and Recruiting:

The Good, the OK, and the Ugly

Recruiters fall into three categories. The following, based on my experience, are descriptions of those three categories.

The Good (Generally Company Recruiters)
- They present themselves and their companies well; they appear professional.
- They represent highly regarded line management; they are not "deadwood."
- They have read your résumé before the interview begins.
- They know all about their company when you ask questions.

The OK (Fee-Based Recruiters)
- Their motivation is to match as many candidates to a job as possible.
- They are more interested in the number of jobs they fill and not whether the recruit closely fits a company's needs.
- They may often "puff up" the job to entice as many applicants as possible.
- They may not have a good grasp of the company and the job's requirements.

The Ugly
- They appeal to the desperate and the naive, particularly those in midcareer or those leaving the military.
- They will have a smooth sales pitch and paint a rosy picture of a person's job prospects.
- They will promise leads to key decision makers and require payment of thousands of dollars up front—beware.

7. The Importance of Good Communications:

Write Well, Speak Well, Look Good

A survey was made of corporate recruiters. More than 90 percent said that what they sought first in a job candidate was the ability to communicate well. Make sure you speak and write well—and look good. Other surveys indicate the primary reason employees are fired is lack of good communication skills.

Write Well

Introductory or cover letters, résumés, reports, and so forth, must be perfect! They should be concise, easy to understand, and provide relevant and factual information. They should be devoid of jargon and have no grammar or spelling errors—*none*.

Take time to prepare all your written communications and then edit, edit, and edit.
- When editing, always use your spelling and grammar checker.
- Use a thesaurus to identify the words that best describe what you mean.
- Read and edit your correspondence slowly—at least two to three times.
- Read each sentence aloud and slowly—word by word.

- Have another person edit your writing; he or she will identify errors you will miss.
- Edit the document immediately after writing it. Then put it aside for two or three days and edit it again; you will find errors you missed in the first edit.

Recruiters and executive search consultants say, "The smallest error may result in your introductory letter or résumé being tossed into the wastebasket—before being read."

Speak Well
- Practice introducing yourself; it should not sound superficial or practiced. Introductions should take no longer than thirty seconds. It can be described as "your elevator speech." Practice it.
- When speaking to a person or a group, eliminate all expressions such as "like," "you know," and so on. It types you as immature or unprofessional.
- When speaking to a group, *speak slowly*—slower than normal. It lets the audience keep up with what you are saying. It also provides "thinking time."
- Good presentations can get you a job and get you promoted. They can also be a one-time experience that will remain in people's mind for a long time—for better or worse.

The following is what others and I consider a good outline for oral presentations:
- Introduce yourself.
- Thank the audience for inviting you to speak to them.
- Begin your presentation with an icebreaker. It can be a joke or a question. Most speakers prefer a question. An example is, "Before I start, how many of you drive a Buick? (Audience raises hands.) How many an Audi?" (Hands raised.)

An icebreaker relaxes the audience, gets their attention, and develops rapport with the speaker.

- Next say, "I am going to talk to you about four things. They are…" and then list the four key points of your presentation. For example, if you are speaking about the recession, you might talk about
  1. how the recession started in 2007;
  2. reasons for the recession;
  3. the negative results of the recession; and
  4. steps taken to prevent future recessions.
- Describe in detail each of the four things.
- Summarize the four things.
- Ask for questions.

If you use PowerPoint slides in the oral presentation, do the following:

- Include simple colorful graphics when appropriate.
- Limit each slide to six bullets.
- Limit each bullet to six words.
- Use simple words.
- Use cue cards; *do not* read from the script on the slide.
- Do not use acronyms that most people will not understand. Learn about the profile of your audience before your presentation. Key your presentation to that profile. As an example, is your audience older, younger, predominately male or female, and so forth?
- Generally, limit the presentation to about thirty minutes.
- Use appropriate hand gestures and body language.
- Keep your eyes on the audience; keep scanning the audience when speaking.

Rehearse, rehearse, and rehearse your speech and your slide presentation.

Look Good

- First impressions are very important. Interviewees make a lasting impression, either positive or negative, within the first five seconds of an interview.
- Remember, you never have a second chance to make a good first impression.
- Have a firm handshake; look the interviewer in the eye.
- Do not slump in the chair.
- Dress equal to or a little better than the interviewer. If interviewing with an agricultural company, consider dressing casually; with a bank, dress formally.
- Hide tattoos; remove face-piercing jewelry.
- Consider reading John T. Molloy's book *New Dress for Success.*
- Don't do stupid stuff—like chewing gum.

8. Information Interviews:

One or Two Things Can Happen—Both Are Good

You are despondent. You have tried everything. You just graduated from college with no job opportunities except with fast-food restaurants. Perhaps you just lost your job and are "in the dumps."

Give yourself a break with information interviews. They are easy to acquire and can provide you information on companies where there may be a job that fits your objectives. You can get good information on a company or industry. You may also identify networking contacts that might find you a job. Information interviews may also relieve a feeling of despondence and improve your morale.

Believe it or not, most people want to help you find a job even when they cannot provide it. That is why most people will be happy to meet for an information interview. It also provides them an opportunity to display their knowledge of the business, and they like to do that. However, they won't meet with you if they think you will press them for a job—a job they don't have.

Who are these people? Suppose you want to work in sales or a sales-related job. The first tier for an information interview might be the neighbor who is an executive with an insurance business, that uncle who is a stockbroker, or the aunt who manages a residential real estate office. The second tier consists of managers or executives you don't know, but who might be responsive to a request for an information interview.

What to Do during an Information Interview

There are things you should and should not do to develop an effective information interview strategy. It involves research, planning, and preparation.

Things You Should Do
- Identify the work you want to do and the people who are doing that kind of work.
- Concentrate on first-tier people; they know you. Focus on second-tier people after you have exhausted the first tier.
- Have a face-to-face interview instead of a telephone interview.
- Develop questions to ask the interviewee. Customize your questions to his or her industry.

Questions for the insurance industry might include the following:
- What are the reasons you decided to work in the insurance business? (Let him or her talk; he or she may do so effusively.)
- What parts of the insurance business do you like the best? Is it selling life insurance, auto insurance, property insurance, or health insurance? Why?
- Why did you decide to work for this insurance company instead of another company?
- What do you believe are the future growth and job opportunities in the insurance business?
- What impact will the government's Affordable Care Act have on the health insurance business?
- What does it take to be a great salesperson in the insurance business?

Things You Should Not Do
Do not directly or indirectly ask the person for a job. Let the interviewee make the offer on his or her own.

In Summary
- Information interviews are much easier to acquire than job interviews.
- Find out as much as you can about the industry before the interview.
- Remember that people want to help if they can.
- Customize your interview questions to the industry the interviewee represents.
- Let the interviewee identify job opportunities with his or her company or other companies.
- After the interview, send the interviewee a thank-you note. Include your customized résumé so that the interviewee will remember you if he or she identifies job opportunities in the future that match your objectives.

9. Networking:

The Hidden Market Where More Than 70 Percent of Jobs Are Found

Networking is one of the least understood and least used of the job-search processes. Few people do it at all, and fewer do it well. However, it's where more than half of all job seekers find jobs. You would be negligent by not using it.

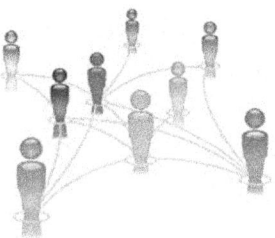

Several years ago I wrote an article on networking that was published in the *National Business Employment Weekly*—at the time a subsidiary of the *Wall Street Journal*. The title of the article was "Networking Is Like Growing a Flower Garden." Some of the key advice in the article remains relevant today:

- Spread your seeds liberally: contact many people.
- Water the seeds carefully: keep your networking contacts in the loop.
- Let the seeds generate new seeds: encourage your network contacts to mention your job-search interests to other people.
- *Do nothing* to destroy the seeds: do not pester your networking contacts. If you do, they may stop helping you.

My Networking Story

It was a drizzly day in San Francisco. There were only five people in the restaurant. About ten feet ahead of me in the line was a man in a black raincoat. He went to sit alone at one of the rectangular tables. I walked to his table and asked, "May I sit with you?" He said, "Please do."

"You look vaguely familiar," I said.

"Perhaps we've seen each other at the Olympic Club," he suggested. (The Olympic Club is an upscale private club in San Francisco. My thought was, "He *is* somebody, and I *am not* a member of the Olympic Club.")

"I don't belong to the Olympic Club," I told him, "but perhaps we've seen each other on the train to San Francisco."

He said, "Yes, I recall now; that's where I've seen you."

I told him I was a district manager with AT&T, and I asked what he did. He said he had a degree in law. I asked if he was with a law firm, and he said, "I was a lawyer for some time, but not anymore."

"Oh," I said. "And what do you do now?"

He said, "Oh, just general administration for a company in San Francisco."

I said, "Oh, who do you work for?"

He said, "California Environmental Products Corporation." (Note this is a fictitious name, which I've shortened to CEP.)

Then I asked, "What job do you have?"

He said, "I'm chairman of the board." He then told me his name and gave me his business card. I was very impressed.

Because I was considering leaving AT&T, I wrote him a letter. I said I was looking for job opportunities in San Francisco that matched my experience. About a week later, I received a phone call from the chairman's administrative assistant, saying that Thomas, vice president of information systems for CEP, would be calling me. Thomas called and invited me to lunch. During lunch, Thomas said, "Bill, I have nothing that would match your experience now, but let's stay in touch and meet for lunch occasionally." We agreed to do so. Shortly thereafter, I accepted a job as the senior telecommunications consultant with another large company in San Francisco.

About three years later, that company divested about 50 percent of its companies and made similar reductions in its corporate staff. My job and many others were eliminated (but I was provided a very nice outplacement package). Shortly thereafter, I called Thomas and said, "Tom, my company is going through a significant downsizing. Might you know of companies in San Francisco that may be interested in a person with my background?" (Note I did not ask him for a job.)

"What's wrong with CEP?" he asked.

I said, "Nothing."

"Well, I've been thinking about replacing my director of telecommunications; he may be interested in retiring early. Would you be interested?" I said yes, and after several interviews, I was offered the job—and I accepted.

Networking is the "hidden job market." All job seekers should tap into it.

Networking Is Key to Finding a Job

- The Manpower Group surveyed 59,133 clients between 2008 and 2010 and concluded that networking was the source of a new job for 41 percent of job seekers in 2008, 45 percent in 2009, and 41 percent in 2010. The remaining jobs were found among six other sources.
- A report from ABC News concluded that 80 percent of jobs were found through networking.
- Another survey concluded that 46 percent of people over fifty found their jobs through networking.
- The president of a career consulting company concluded that just sending out résumés, even hundreds of them, in response to ads probably won't help that much. The reason, he said, is that "most jobs aren't posted or advertised."
- The president of another career consulting company concluded that at least *70 percent, if not 80 percent, of jobs are not published.* And yet most people—about 70 or 80 percent—are spending their time surfing the net instead of getting out there and talking to employers.

Guidelines to Effective Networking

Talk to People

Networking is the building of alliances. It's not contacting everyone you know, nor is it making cold calls to people you do not know.

- Start by preparing a list of possible network contacts among people you know.
- Prepare business cards that give a very brief description of the work you seek and how you can be contacted. Distribute them generously.

- Visit with your neighbors or friends; tell them what you are looking for.
- Strike up conversations with people you do not know.
- Include people who may interact with those who may be able to help you.
- Maintain your list of network contacts. You may need it tomorrow.
- Routinely talk with people who are currently working in your field. *Twenty-seven percent of all new hires are made from referrals.*

A list of network contacts could include the following:
- relatives, friends, and neighbors
- alumni, former coworkers, or previous bosses
- your doctor, dentist, barber, hairdresser, or gardener
- your college professors or instructors

You may question why your doctor, hairdresser, or gardener are on the list. That is because they may have a client or customer who is looking for someone with your experience and education. You would be surprised who knows whom.

Use the Internet
A phenomenon of the twenty-first century are employment web-sites and a variety of social networks. With the evolution of the Internet, many new job-search opportunities have developed.
- *LinkedIn:* LinkedIn is an excellent choice for a college student or a young professional. My friends believe using LinkedIn is the best way to find a job.
- *Monster.com:* Monster provides excellent advice on the job-search process and current information on available jobs.
- *Career Builder:* Career Builder provides information on avail-able jobs and alerts when new jobs are made available.

- *Other job sites:* Explore other smaller, web-based organizations that provide similar services.

However, you should not splatter your résumé to all those organizations. Carefully identify only those that best fit your needs, and they should not be a substitute for the other recommendations provided in this book.

10.

An Internship That Gets You to the Head of the Job Line after You Graduate

Acquiring an internship is one of the best ways to get a job after graduation.

Some Facts about Internships

- The most prestigious internships are difficult to acquire. As an example, in summer 2013, Goldman-Sachs hired 350 interns from 17,000 applicants. Fortunately, that does not represent the vast majority of internships.
- Sixty-one percent of students who had internships received job offers by the end of their senior year.
- Many summer internships are with the federal government:
  - In summer 2014, the Speaker of the House of Representatives hired 24 unpaid interns.
  - The members of the House and Senate hired more than 6,000 interns.
  - The White House hired 429 interns in 2013.
  - The Supreme Court has its own internship program.
  - Each summer, 20,000 to 40,000 interns work in Washington, DC, government departments.
- If you want to research federal job opportunities, go to the web page: federal government internships summer 2015. It provides information on many federal departments including the Department of State, the White House, the CIA, and the FBI. Internships with many of these agencies will look great on any résumé and broaden your knowledge of the world.

- The Big Four accounting firms hired about 30,000 interns in 2014.
- The following industries hire a significant number of interns. In order, they are
  1. accounting—primarily, but not exclusively, the Big Four;
  2. oil and energy;
  3. investment banking;
  4. public relations and communications;
  5. law;
  6. apparel and fashion;
  7. hospitality;
  8. government; and
  9. publishing.

Acquire a Summer Internship before Graduation

Career centers may help you identify an internship. However, if you are interested in a particular company, call that company. You may be surprised; the company may establish an internship for you just because you called. There are upsides and a few downsides to internships. Nonetheless, if you cannot acquire a summer job, you should accept an internship to learn about a business and to help you acquire a job after graduation. In addition, internships look great on a résumé.

Cons

Some internships pay relatively well, but many pay nothing, and an internship may not necessarily lead to a full-time, paid position. A young woman worked for one year in an unpaid internship for an advertising company in San Francisco. At the end of the year, they told her they no longer needed her. So be careful with "glamorous" internships where the demand is low and the supply almost infinite.

Pros

- Internships can pave the way to a full-time job after graduation.
- Through an internship, you can learn something about a specific job or industry.
- It will improve your résumé, which will make it more appealing to future possible employers.
- You will broaden your network contacts.

Internships are an excellent way to "leap to the head of the pack." All students should try to get an internship before their junior or senior years. Just be cautious and enter into the agreement with your eyes wide open. Don't get "milked" for free labor.

11.

Introductory Letters That Get the Attention of the Hiring Manager

"Clunk" is the noise that a poorly written introductory letter makes when it's tossed into a wastebasket. You don't want your introductory letter and résumé to go there.

How do you get past the heap of cover letters and résumés that pile up in the human resources department— often thousands of them? It's not easy. Some companies do not even look at résumés, but have them scanned for key words.

Flooding companies with a massive amount of introductory letters and résumés does not work. Preparing correspondence that may open the door to a job opportunity requires hard work and research. It also requires matching a specific hiring manager's real or unrecognized needs with your qualifications and accomplishments. How do you do that?

Crafting an Effective Cover Letter
This is an example of what *not* to do.

> **Dear Sir or Ms.:**
>
> I want to work for XYZ Corporation. My résumé is attached.
>
> Thank you for your consideration.
>
> Sylvia Patterson

If you send that introductory or cover letter, it will go clunk—count on it!

First, understand what drives job opportunities. It's not that a company is a good corporate citizen or charitable. It's because it wants to make a profit and has problems to solve. *Companies want problem solvers.*

You can identify business problem opportunities by canvassing one of many business periodicals that are published in many cities. A good example is the *San Jose Business Journal*. The *Journal* includes executive profiles and business leads. It also includes a section called "People on the Move," which identifies managers who are moving into or out of jobs or are moving to the San Jose area to establish a new sales office, distribution facility, and so forth.

The following is a good guideline on how to proceed:
* Do not send your introductory or cover letter to personnel or human resources. Identify the name of the prospective hiring manager and send it directly to him or her.
  * The first paragraph should identify a problem or situation the hiring manager may have. As an example, a company may be establishing a new sales office in San Antonio.

- o The second paragraph should explain how you might have solved a similar problem in the past. Be specific; provide facts and data.
- o The third paragraph should try to establish a personal connection to the reader. Identify a person, organization, school, or sport that you have in common with the reader. The objective is to dissuade the hiring manager's administration assistant from taking your introductory letter and résumé and making it go clunk.
- Follow up with, "I will call your office shortly to see if you are interested in talking to me."

Put yourself in the shoes of the hiring manager of a company. He or she is busy. The telephone rings often; e-mails flood in; the appointment book is full. The manager has objectives to meet, problems to solve. Then comes the mail. There is a note from his or her boss, budget reports to evaluate—and a few introductory letters with attached résumés. The first cover letter starts, "To whom it may concern" (clunk); the second letter starts, "I seek employment to broaden my managerial skills" (clunk). Then the manager receives the following introductory letter.

Mr. David Benbow
Vice President Sales
Century Semiconductor
1800 Connaught Drive
San Jose, CA

Dear Mr. Benbow:

An article in the *San Jose Mercury* said Century Semiconductor is opening a new sales office in San Jose. The article also said you are looking for twelve salespersons.

I am an experienced semiconductor salesperson. I won the Salesman of the Year award for Signal Semiconductor in Dallas in 2009. During that period, I added twenty accounts to the Dallas office.

The article said that you graduated from the School of Business at Cornell in 1993 and belonged to Kappa Sigma men's social fraternity. I was also a Kappa Sig at Cornell and graduated in 2013.

I will call your office shortly to discuss a sales opportunity with Century Semiconductor; my résumé is attached.

I look forward to meeting you.

Sincerely,

Harold Johnson

Compare this introductory or cover letter to the one previously illustrated. Which do you think has the better chance of getting an interview?

12.

Résumés That Make a Recruiter Salivate

Résumés all provide the same information— chronological, functional, and targeted—but present it in different formats. There are many kinds of résumés; however, most do not highlight the information that is most important to the recruiter.

The Importance of the Job Objective

Put yourself in the shoes of a recruiter. He or she has jobs to fill. They want to fill them as easily as possible. First, they want to know what the applicant wants to do, which should be covered in the job objective. However, the job objectives on many résumés are long-winded, self-aggrandizing gibberish.

The following job objective illustrates what I mean. A job objective like the one below simply frustrates a recruiter because he or she has no clue as to what kind of work the applicant wishes to do. The recruiter can't take the time to sort it out or may not be qualified to do so.

> **Job Objective**
>
> I seek a job with a progressive company that will provide me with the opportunity to reach my full potential. I want a job where I can work effectively with people and have the opportunity to display my excellent communications skills in sales, marketing, personnel, and related areas.

A recruiter wants to know "what and where." Make the job objective clear, concise, and customized to the job available; it should be limited to eighteen words.

> **Job Objective**
>
> A job as a teller with Wells Fargo in Monterey County, leading to a branch manager position.

Describe Your Accomplishments

There is only one reason why companies hire people: it's because they have problems to solve. There is no other reason. That's why the second most important part of the résumé should be a description of an applicant's accomplishments. Those accomplishments should be related to the résumé's job objective. Accomplishments should, as much as possible, include an introductory action verb, a measurement of performance, and a time boundary.

You may think you do not have accomplishments that are related to your job objective, but think hard—something about your accomplishments in leadership or other areas may be of interest to the recruiter.

The following provides examples of accomplishments related to the job objective of bank teller. It also lists other accomplishments that may be of interest to the recruiter.

Accomplishments Related to the Job Objective

- Received more letters of commendation than any other intern while working during summer 2012 at the Wells Fargo branch in Carmel.
- Received Intern of the Month award from the Wells Fargo branch at Pebble Beach in July 2013.
- Implemented a new software system at the Wells Fargo branch at Pebble Beach during my summer internship in July 2013.

Other Related Accomplishments

- Led the team that received the highest grade in the managerial accounting class project at California State University–Monterey Bay during spring semester 2013.
- Was president of Delta Sigma Theta Sorority during the fall and spring semesters of 2012.

Résumé Tips
- Your résumé should generally not exceed one page.
- Prepare an accomplishment-focused résumé that is crisp and easy to read and quickly grabs a recruiter's attention.
- *Customize* your résumé to fit the company you are interviewing. A generic résumé will lose out to a customized résumé nine times out of ten.
- Large companies may not read your résumé; optical character reading, a system that looks for key words (e.g., sales, marketing, software), may scan it.

- Use this to your advantage by inserting key words in your résumé; for example, words that you saw in the job advertisement.
- Mirror those key words in your cover letter to the recruiter.

Other parts of a résumé may be of interest to a recruiter, such as
- awards;
- work experience;
- courses taken; and
- educational background.

The most important parts of the résumé are the Job Objective and Accomplishments. The "other parts may be of interest" and sometimes appropriate. *However*, they are not what a recruiter will focus on.

13.

Job Interviews That Make or Break You

The interview is the culmination of the job-search process. The introductory letter and résumé can be perfect, but all that hard work can be destroyed by a bad interview. Conversely, an excellent interview can often overcome a mediocre or poor introductory letter and résumé.

Understand that the recruiter is generally only a screener—a "stop or go" person. Seldom is the recruiter the decision maker. If you pass through that screen, companies will often schedule you for a formal job interview, which could be one interview with your prospective manager and/or a series of interviews with other people in the company.

Interviewing well is a skill that can be developed only through many interviews, feedback, and repetition. If you do not prepare well and just try to breeze through it, your interview may end in disaster.

Job interviews often depend upon the size of the company and the importance they place on recruiting high-quality people. Both Procter & Gamble and AT&T are companies where I spent a full day in interviews before a job was offered.

Prepare Well for the Interview

The most important thing to remember about the final job interview is *preparation, preparation, and preparation.*

- Learn as much as you can about the company before the interview. Use Google and other search engines.
- Interviewers love interviewees who have researched the company before the interview. Few interviewees do so, and it will place you ahead of the pack if you do.
- If you are not asked a question that you are prepared to answer, find an opportunity to include the issue in the interview.
- Determine the appropriate dress. Some companies have multiple interviews with executives in "carpet land." Carpet land interviews generally require a suit or sports jacket and tie.
- Find out as much as you can about the people who will be interviewing you; the recruiter may be able to tell you. If not, you may find out something about the interviewers from a Google search. Use that information to make statements or ask questions like
  - I notice we both went to school at UCLA and both received a degree in economics.
  - I understand Acme's revenues increased 20 percent last year. How did Acme do that?

- You may be asked one or more of the ten most asked interview questions. Be prepared in advance to provide good answers. The following are what I believe to be the most important interview questions, roughly in order of importance:
  - Why do you want to work for this company?
  - What do you know about the company?
  - What were your most important accomplishments in college or on a job?
  - What do you think you can contribute to the company?

o What are your greatest strengths?
o What was your major in college and why did you choose it?
o Where do you expect to be in five years?

Think about potential questions before the interview and have your answers ready.

Some books recommend generic answers; I recommend that you do not respond generically. Your answer should be how *you* want to answer the question, not with a recommended answer.

My experience: I recall the first question the recruiter from IBM asked a recruit (a day when my recruiting cubicle was next to IBM's). It was, "Tell me what you know about IBM." If the recruit had not researched the company and was unable to respond, he or she left the IBM booth shortly after the start of the interview. Don't let that happen to you. *Be prepared* for the interview.

Interview Tips

- When you introduce yourself, have a firm handshake and make direct eye contact. Remember that you cannot make a good second first impression. The interviewer's impression of you can be made in the first five or ten seconds after you meet him or her.
- If the interviewer asks a question such as "How did you do that?" it's a good sign. Describe your accomplishments in "living color." Make the interviewer visualize it.
- Do not initiate a discussion on a possible salary in the job interview. If the interviewer asks what salary you wish, provide a range. Questions about salary and compensation may indicate you are more interested in the salary than the job, which can be a turnoff. Leave it for later.

- At the end of the interview, if the interviewer does not provide feedback on your prospects of your getting the job, ask for it. Use that feedback to find out where you stand. It also better prepares you for the next interview.
- The interviewer is primarily interested in what you *have done* instead of what you *think you can do*. Be prepared with several accomplishment-based stories.
- The interviewer is not interested in your self-evaluation or "who you are." The interviewer will determine that for him- or herself.
- *Do not* provide inaccurate or incomplete information. People have been fired many years after they have been hired because information on their résumé turned out to be false.
- If you are interested in the job, send a letter or e-mail to the people who interviewed you. Tell them you enjoyed meeting them and are interested in joining the company. Few recruits do that today. Those who do will differentiate themselves from the pack.

14. Fifty and Fired:

Is It a Dilemma or an Opportunity? It's Your Choice

I wrote an article several years ago titled, "Fired at 50: One Executive's Story." It was about being fired in middle age. It was published in the *National Business Employment Weekly*, previously a subsidiary of the *Wall Street Journal*. The article reviewed thirteen lessons learned from my surprise termination. The following describes what happened to me and the lessons I learned. Less than four months after being fired, I found a better job that paid more.

My Story
When I entered my boss's office, I could see only his profile. He was backlit by the bright sun streaming through the window behind him. Behind the window was a gorgeous view of the San Francisco Bay and the Golden Gate Bridge—what a wonderful view and day.

He began by talking about the accomplishments I had achieved for the company. (I thought, "Hmm, bonus time?") Then he started talking about how the company had divested itself of almost 50 percent of its subsidiary companies. (I thought, "Smart idea," because it might help the value of my options.)

Then he said that the company had a policy of downsizing corporate staff at the same percentage as the companies they no longer held. (I thought it was a smart idea; it made sense to me.)

Then he said the downsizing would affect my employment with the company. (I thought, "Did I hear that right?")

Finally, he said, "Bill, unfortunately, effective November 1, you will no longer be employed by the company." The date was three months from our meeting. (I thought, "*Oh my*—fifty and fired. What will I do now?")

He went on to say I would receive six months' severance pay and outplacement services, and he would provide a positive reference letter whenever I requested it. (At the time I was in a fog and hardly heard what he said.) Fortunately, being terminated that way, in comparison with other companies, was considerate and helpful. Also fortunately, I found a new and better job before my severance package ran out.

What to Do
Other companies, particularly in Silicon Valley many years ago, were far less gentle. The worst-case story involves a semiconductor firm. The firm allegedly made the following announcement on a Friday at noon on the company's address system: "Please listen to the following message. Effective today, the following employees will be terminated: John Abbot, Mary Christopher, and Peter Christopher. Please pick up your last check at the personnel office at 4:00 p.m. today and submit your ID card. You will also be provided a package that describes your individual severance pay." That was it.

The result is the same. You have been downsized, made redundant—all synonyms for being fired.

So what do you do, particularly if you are over fifty? Options include

1. becoming angry, threatening to sue the company, or finding solace in a gin bottle—all counterproductive;
2. taking a few days to gain perspective and considering that this may be an opportunity to experience better days ahead— "Forget the old, look forward to the new."

I suggest option two. But how do you do that? I remember the words of advice I received from a highly regarded Silicon Valley executive search consultant. He said, "This may be the time for you to dream a few dreams."

Specifically:
* If the company provides outplacement center services as part of your termination package, *use it*—right away. Many can provide excellent advice, job-search resources, and a shoulder to lean on when things look bleak. They also provide an opportunity to network with others using the outplacement center and a place to go to each day instead of moping around the house.
* Think, "If I knew when I first started work what I know now, would I make the same decision?" If not, perhaps you should pursue a different path to find a new job.
* Turn your avocation into your new vocation. A company told a friend after a demotion that his career was limited and his opportunity days with the company were finished. Over the years he had enjoyed taking pictures of weekend weddings,

so he decided to start his own photography business. He eventually made good money and was as "happy as a clam."

- Consider starting your own consulting business. Companies often want an experienced (read: gray-haired) consultant to help them during peak times or when they need expertise, but for only a few months at a time. When I established my consulting company, my slogan was "Rent a Director of Tele-communications." I did consulting work for banks, hospitals, high-tech companies, and other enterprises. I billed the companies twice my hourly rate with my previous company.
- Retire. Many people, however, find that they must stay busy doing something challenging and interesting. Retirement for some can be boring.

15. Jobs:

How to Keep One, and When and How to Leave One

If you have a job, how do you keep it? If you want to leave a job, how do you do it without creating problems? There are things you should and should not do.

How to Keep Your Job
Things You Should Do
- Work hard and intelligently.
- Contribute positively toward meeting your boss's objectives.
- Have a positive attitude toward your boss and the company.
- Make your boss's job easier. Offer to do work that the boss does not have the time or inclination to do. Some call it "taking a monkey off the boss's back."
- If you are dissatisfied with the boss's policies, do not discuss it in a group setting. Discuss those issues privately with your boss behind closed doors.
- Be a team player.

Things You Should Not Do
- Do not try to put "your monkey" on your boss's back.
- Do not be disruptive, negative, or a complainer.
- Do not try to schmooze your boss.

When and How to Leave a Job

There will be times when you should consider leaving a job.

- If your company is on the rocks, or if events will likely require a significant downsizing, particularly if the downsizing may affect your job, it may be time to leave. You want to be pro-active instead of just hoping for the best and being reactive. Start looking for a new job well before there are forced lay-offs, early retirement packages, or similar inducements. Take action to be the first out the door while jobs in your field with other companies exist. If you wait too long, people who were forced to leave the company before you may crowd the job market in your field.
- You may have been told your time is up because there is a mismatch between your skills and interests and your job's requirements. In the past, HP and IBM tried to find a better fit for mismatched employees or simply put some employees on the shelf until retirement. Unfortunately, in the twenty-first century, most companies can no longer afford to do this.
- You may have offended a senior manager and may have "poisoned your well." You can try to have a frank discussion with that manager to see if there is anything you can do to take the poison out of the well.

How Best to Leave a Job

The best way to leave a job is to first find another job that better meets your objectives. Examples of work situations that are more satisfactory could include

- finding a firm that is growing quickly in a fast-growing industry; and
- finding a job that offers a promotion and increased responsibility with a better income.

Things You Should Consider

- Do not leave your current job if you are in the middle of a critical project, important sales proposal, and so forth. Discuss a date with the company you work for so that your departure does not create a negative impact on the company you are leaving. *Do not* leave them "in the lurch."
- Make sure your company understands why you are leaving; otherwise, they may assume you are leaving because you are dissatisfied.
- Do not leave a job before you find another job. Some companies may provide two to three months on the job before you are terminated. Others may not; if so, request it. Your company would be remiss to not consider it. No company wants former employees out in the street waving a sign or seeing the company maligned in a local newspaper. In addition, no company wants to be taken to court in today's litigious society.
- Leave the job with your "flags flying high."
- Communicate to others that in the long run, it may have been the best thing that happened to you.
- Do not thrash around and become bitter and dejected. Look forward, not backward.

And finally, if you receive bad news, do not go home and kick the dog or yell at your soul mate (or vice versa). Either action could be highly counterproductive.

16.

Executive Summary

The following summarizes the key points in this book. Use it as a quick and simple reminder of the most important issues.

> **Executive Summary**

- Companies and job opportunities have changed dramatically since the end of the twentieth century. You must change how you look for a job to capitalize on those opportunities.
- Get a good grasp on what you want to do *before you start your job search*. If not, you will waste time and money.
- Start your job search with networking. That is where about 70 percent of all jobs are found. It's often referred to as the "hidden job market."
- Use the information interview process to learn more about jobs in an industry and maybe even find a job.
- Write well, speak well, and look good. All written communications must be perfect. Learn to make first-class presentations and speak well. Remember that you have only one chance to make a good first impression. If the first impression is bad, you may not be able to recover from it.
- Write a customized introductory letter that gets the attention of the hiring manager. Do not send out a flood of unfocused introductory letters and accompanying résumés to human resources departments. Use a rifle and not a shotgun.
- Focus on the two most important parts of your résumé:

1. a concise, focused job objective that does not exceed eighteen words.
2. a list of your accomplishments that matches the objective of the job. Each accomplishment should start with an action verb, be measurable, and indicate the period during which you accomplished it.

- Research, research, and research before your job interview. Know the company better than the recruiter. Prepare your answers to the most asked questions before the interview.
- If you get fired in midcareer, don't despair. Remain positive. Think creatively. Do not consider only the jobs you have held before (they often no longer exist). Find new opportunities that better fit your interests. Do not try to find solace in a gin bottle; it will just make things worse.

About the Author

Bill Meyer was born in Nashville, Tennessee. Bill and his parents moved to St. Louis, Missouri, shortly thereafter, but he later moved to and graduated from the Alton High School in Alton, Illinois. He began his college education at Purdue University, but he soon left Purdue to accept a Regular Naval Officers Training Corps Scholarship at the University of Missouri. He graduated from Missouri with a BS and MS in industrial engineering.

Bill's navy experience transformed his life. Three summer midshipman cruises, which took him to Europe, the West Coast, and Hawaii, changed his perspective on the world from very narrow to very wide. As a naval officer on the aircraft carrier USS *Coral Sea*, he also visited many countries in Asia. Bill also served as Officer of the Deck for Carrier Task Force Operations.

After the navy, he spent more than thirty-five years in telecommunications systems and services management and consulting. He worked at AT&T, Seagate Technology, Transamerica, PG & E, and Andersen and Gartner Consulting and as an independent consultant. Shortly after he left the business world, in semiretirement, he taught business ethics at San Francisco State University. He subsequently taught business communications at California

State University–Monterey Bay. He was president of two men's clubs, one in the city of Monterey and the other in Pebble Beach.

Bill's love for writing began in the ninth grade when he extemporaneously wrote a poem during study hall, titled, "The Champion," which was published in the school yearbook. He was hooked. He has written articles about searching for a job in the *National Business Employment Weekly* and many business and consulting reports and articles about telecommunications. He wrote an article about becoming a father again at age forty-five called, "No, He Is Not Our Grandson," which was published in *Babytalk* magazine. He also wrote *My Story*, a 150-page memoir.

Bill lives in Pebble Beach with his wife. He has three children and three grandchildren.

www.ingramcontent.com/pod-product-compliance
Lightning Source LLC
Chambersburg PA
CBHW071303170526
45165CB00003B/1395